CO[URSE]
1619

CURRICULUM

WHEN RACISM BEGAN IN AMERICA

GRADES 6-12

DR. JAWANZA KUNJUFU

African American IMAGES

LIST OF ILLUSTRATIONS AND SOURCES

1   Trayvon Martin, 2012.

2   Jack Delano, Farmers Café, with separate entrances for Whites and Blacks, 1940. Library of Congress. https://www.loc.gov/pictures/item/2017747555/

3   Crowd smiles at lynching of Lige Daniels, 1920, from *Without Sanctuary: Lynching Photography in America*, James Allen, et al., eds. (Sante Fe, NM: Twin Palms Publishers, 2000).

4   Emmett Till in an open casket, August 1955, *Chicago Defender* Archives.

5   George Floyd's murder, May 25, 2020, Witness camera.

6   Four girls killed in bombing at 16th Street Baptist Church, Birmingham, September 15, 1963. National Park Service.

7   Poster of Willie H. West Minstrel Show (Reproduction), Cincinnati: Strobridge Lithographing Company, 1900.

8   Bloody Sunday – Police attack protesters at Pettus Bridge, 1965. https://www.politico.com/story/2018/03/07/this-day-in-politics-march/7-1965-437394

9   George Floyd's murder, May 25, 2020, Witness camera.

TEACHER AND STUDENT READ THIS PAGE TOGETHER

Does your teacher say, "I don't see color. I see children as children."

Does your teacher make negative comments about children of color?

Does your teacher lower expectations base on race, gender, income or appearance?

Does your teacher ignore, tolerate, have disdain for or fear students of color?

Does the classroom décor motivate students of color?

Does your teacher give more criticisms than praises?

Does your teacher admit that race is a factor?

Does your teacher understand Black history and culture?

Does your teacher appreciate Black history and culture?

I am writing this book because I love and respect you. Eighty- four percent of Blacks believe racism is the major reason for their lack of progress. Only 54 percent of Whites feel the same.[1] Racism is an evil spirit. People who are secure are comfortable with differences. People who are insecure believe because they are different it makes them better.

Are you secure? Are you comfortable with differences? People who are racist, try to convince other people they are inferior. Think about this: If you were inferior why discriminate? If you were inferior shouldn't racists be open to a fair contest? Do not let anyone convince you that you are inferior. Do not ever believe someone is better than you. You are a gift from above!

How many people live in the world? Almost eight billion.[2] Do you believe you can divide eight billion people into three races? What are the three races? Black, White and Asian. Their scientific names are Negroid, Caucasoid and Mongoloid.

What is the difference between a race and an ethnic group? Where do we place Latinx, Native Americans, Arabs, Indians, Jews, Pacific Islanders and many more? Is race biological and ethnicity sociological? Are there three races and six ethnic groups?

If someone is sick and they need a blood transfusion or an organ, do you think they only want the blood or organ from one race or ethnic group? We are all part of one race—the human race!

People who are insecure believe their race or ethnic group is better than all others. They will do whatever it takes to promote their race or group. They will also do whatever it takes to prevent other races or groups from improvement.

What happens when people marry outside of their race and have a child? To which race or ethnic group does the child belong?

Have you ever heard of the "one drop rule?"[3] In the United States, Whites were in the majority and did not need an increase in population, therefore when White President Thomas Jefferson had sex with his Black mistress Sally Hemings their offspring would be labeled Black because the baby had more than one drop of Black blood.

In Central and South America, where Whites were in the minority, Whites decided one drop of White blood would make you White.

There are thousands of Blacks who are passing for White. Why do they want to be White? Why would they deny their Black ancestors and relatives? Are you proud to be Black?

There are almost eight billion people in the world. What percent are White? Do you think Whites are the majority? They are only 12 percent of the population.[4] They are less than one billion. There are more Blacks and Asians. They are the majority in the world. In the United States, Whites are becoming the minority. How do you think that makes Whites feel?

Remember people who are insecure tell themselves they are better than others. People who are secure are comfortable with differences.

What makes someone have dark skin, Black hair and dark color eyes? Melanin. I want you to do research on melanin. I want you to write a paper. The more melanin you have the darker your skin, hair and eye color.

COVID 1619 CURRICULUM

Why do some Blacks dislike their dark skin? Why do some Whites spend hours trying to get a suntan? Why do some Blacks dislike the width of their nose? Why do some Blacks think their lips are too big?

Did your school ever teach you the benefits of dark skin?[5] First, the darker you are the less chance of skin cancer. Second, the darker you are the less chance of sunburn. Third, it delays the aging process. Last, the more sun you can absorb the more vitamin D is produced in your body, which has major health benefits.

What is good hair? If you know what good hair is then you know what bad hair is. Do you have good hair? What are pretty eyes? Do you have pretty eyes? Do you like the color of your skin?

Have you ever watched a music video with dark-skinned females with short hair fully dressed? Racism wants you to believe light skinned females with long straight hair and light colored eyes are prettier.

Have you heard of the doll test?[6] Have you heard of the brown bag test? Psychologists in 1954 showed Black children a dark-skinned and a light skinned doll. Which one did they choose? They chose the light skinned doll. They repeated the study this year and found the same results. Why?

The brown bag test is similar.[7] There were some Black sororities, colleges and organizations that denied admission if you were darker than a brown bag.

This is self-hatred. This is a result of racism.

What is your definition of prejudice?

What is your definition of discrimination?

What is your definition of racism?

Prejudice is when you do not like someone for various reasons that may not be correct. It also gives you stereotypes about a group. When you are prejudiced you think all Black people are loud, violent, good dancers and play basketball very well. A prejudiced person believes Whites are better in science and Blacks are better in sports. They believe Whites are better in math and Blacks are better in music. They also believe Whites are better in reading and Blacks are better in rap.

Are you prejudiced? Do you think that way? Are you good in science, math and reading? What were your grades in these subjects?

Discrimination is when you combine prejudice with unfairness. Let me offer some examples. You have a gym class of 10 students. You choose your team to play basketball. There are five Whites and five Blacks. The two captains only choose members of their race. Some players wanted to play on the other team.

You are having lunch in the cafeteria. You notice all the Blacks are sitting in one section and all the Whites are sitting in another. You would like to sit with the other race, but they will not let you.

There is a school party. Blacks are not happy that the majority of the music features White artists.

```
Prejudice + discrimination + power = racism
```

Does racism exist in your school? Please provide three examples.

Why do some schools suspend, expel and deny participation in their graduation if their hair is natural, braided, has twists, dreadlocks, cornrows or other Black hairstyles? This is racism.

A Black and White student are fighting. The White person started the fight. The school gives the White student a warning and the Black student is suspended for five days. Black students are twice as likely as White students to be suspended. Blacks are 17 percent of the students but constitute 33 of school arrests. Whites are 50 percent of the students but are only 34 percent of school arrests.[8] This is racism.

Some White teachers lower their expectations based on race. They say they do not see color, but they call on Black students less, give more criticisms, ask easier questions, engage and probe less and seldom are in close proximity.

A research study was done with White teachers and Black and White students. The teachers were asked to observe challenging behavior. The majority of the teachers immediately looked at Black male students. The study showed all the students were acting very well. This is racism.

The late Malcolm X was born Malcolm Little. He was an 8th grade honor student. His teacher Mr. Ostrowski asked Malcolm what would he like to become? Malcolm said, "A lawyer." His teacher scolded him and said, "You are a nigger and you can't be a lawyer. Try being a carpenter."[9] This is racism.

A school has 500 students. One hundred are White and 400 are Black. There are three floors in the school. Two hundred Blacks are on the first floor. The classes are special education and remedial. The second floor is also all-Black. Average classes are offered on this floor. The third floor is all-White. These classes include gifted and talented, honors, and advanced placement. In order to be in these classes, you must receive a recommendation. Very few Blacks are recommended and those that are do not feel welcomed. This is racism.

Schools can be in the same state, city and ZIP code, but receive different levels of funding. On average, White schools receive $1,600 more per student annually.[10] In most White schools every teacher has a master's degree. The school has computers in every class. They have a well stocked library, science lab, gymnasium, auditorium and cafeteria. They have a counselor, social worker, nurse and psychologist.

In many Black schools, most teachers lack master's degrees. Many instructors are trying to teach math and science, but they did not major in college in either subject. The school only has 20 computers and they are in one room. They do not have a science lab. They do not have a librarian, counselor, nurse, social worker or psychologist. They do have three police officers. They use the gymnasium as their auditorium and cafeteria. This is racism.

What month/s does your school teach Black history? White history? Why do Blacks get the shortest month and Whites the entire school year?

What is the definition of a continent? Are there seven continents? Is Europe surrounded by water?

Did Abraham Lincoln free the slaves or save the Union? What is the difference between the Emancipation Proclamation and the Thirteenth Amendment?

Did Columbus discover America? Was he the first person in America? What about the Native Americans?

Is Hippocrates the father of medicine? I want you to read his oath. He acknowledges the first doctor came from Egypt. His Greek name was Aesculapius and his African name was Imhotep.

I want you to read and write about Imhotep and the first pyramids until you are convinced you are just as talented in science as sports.

Racism exists beyond schools. It involves our entire society. There is a national program that uses racial testers.[11] There are two testers. One is White and the other is Black. They are both looking for a job and are interviewed by the same White employer. The Black client has a college degree. The White client only has a high school diploma and has a criminal record. Guess who got the job? Why? Unemployment is twice as high in the Black community. When applying online, Blacks are encouraged to use White-sounding names. Why?

The two testers go back to the employer with a videotape of the interview and show the tape. The employer denies he is racist.

The same two testers proceed to a real estate agent to secure a house. The Black client is shown 18 percent fewer houses and they are in poorer neighborhoods. The White client is shown more and better houses. Why?

The testers go back to the agent and show the videotape. The agent denies she is racist.

The testers then go to a bank to secure a business loan. The Black client is denied and the White client is accepted. Whites have a three times greater chance of securing a business loan over Blacks. The testers return to the bank and show the videotape. The loan officer denies he is racist.

Whites have 90 percent of the wealth in America.[12] Blacks have less than 3 percent. The average White has $171,000 in wealth. The average Black only has $17,000 in wealth. This is racism.

Blacks are only 13 percent of America's population, but are over 40 percent of the prison population.[13] Blacks are incarcerated five times greater than Whites.

Blacks and Whites were both in possession of drugs. The judge gave the White person a warning and the Black person five years. Sound familiar? Schools did the same with the school fight.

There is also racism in our media. They show more photos of Black murderers. They show the human side of White murderers. Seventy-two percent of Black males shown on television news are either athletes or criminals. Eighty-two percent of television news producers are White.

These two sets of pictures are everything you need to know about race, crime and media bias.

Racism also exists in our doctors' offices. Research documents 67 percent of doctors have bias against Black patients.[14] They also believe Blacks can tolerate more pain.

Racism is running rampant in our police department.[15] Blacks are stopped three times more often than Whites. Blacks are killed by the police 21 times greater than Whites. Since 2005, only ninety-three officers have been arrested. Only thirty-five have been convicted and less than five have done prison time.

Blacks keep saying, "I can't breathe." White police officers keep saying to juries, "I feared for my life."

I want you to read more about racial police brutality. I want you to provide five or more solutions to this problem. This must stop!

DRIVING WHILE BLACK

On July 6, 2016, Philando Castile was driving in Minnesota with his wife and daughter. The police stopped him and asked to see his license and proof of ownership. He asked for permission to go to his glove department to provide the items. The police shot and killed him. His wife videotaped the entire murder while consoling her daughter.

THE CONVERSATION BETWEEN BLACK PARENTS AND THEIR CHILDREN

Black parents have to tell their children how to respond to the police when they are stopped. They tell them to be polite and respectful. Your life is at risk. They tell them to keep their hands visible. They tell them to ask for permission to move their hands to secure their license and proof of ownership. They tell them even if the police are disrespectful and call them a nigger, they need to be polite. Your life is at stake.

White parents do not need to have this conversation with their children. This is White privilege. What do you suggest we do so that no parents will have to have this conversation?

EATING SKITTLES WHILE BLACK

(Fig. 2, Source: Biography.com)

Trayvon Martin was only 17 years old. He had a bright future. On February 26, 2012, he was walking home after buying some candy from the store. A White man thought Trayvon looked dangerous. The man shot and killed him and pleaded self-defense. Florida and other states have a law called "stand your ground." The court ruled in the man's favor. I want you to write a letter to Trayvon and mail it to his parents. I want you to research and write a paper on the stand your ground law.

RUNNING WHILE BLACK

Ahmaud Arbery was 25 years old. He had a bright future ahead of him. He was going for his daily run in Georgia. Two White men shot and killed him on February 23, 2020.

SITTING IN YOUR APARTMENT WHILE BLACK

Breonna Taylor was 26 years of age. She lived in Louisville. She was a brilliant medical technician. She was sitting on her sofa when three police officers with a no-knock search warrant barged in and shot her eight times on March 13, 2020. I want you to research the outcome of this case.

SHOPPING WHILE BLACK

TRYING TO GET A TAXI WHILE BLACK

WAITING FOR SERVICE IN A RESTAURANT WHILE BLACK

BEING VIEWED AS A WORKER IN AN UPSCALE ESTABLISHMENT WHILE BLACK

SWIMMING IN A HOTEL POOL WHILE BLACK

DRIVING OR WALKING IN A GATED COMMUNITY WHILE BLACK

PLAYING IN THE PARK WHILE BLACK

WEARING ANYTHING WITH BLACK LIVES MATTER VISIBLE

PROTESTING WHILE BLACK = FELONY

PROTESTING WHILE WHITE = MISDEMEANOR

I WANT YOU TO ADD MORE

Racism is expressed in many forms. Whites took oil, gold, diamonds and much more from Africa. Whites have stolen over a trillion dollars. They took eleven million Blacks from Africa and sold them in South and Central America. They took one million Blacks to the United States.[16] Whites made Blacks work for free from 1619 to 1865. There were almost five million Blacks in America in 1865. They were free with no money, land, housing, education or employment.

From 1865 to 1965, we were paid less wages and denied the opportunity to vote. They created separate schools, parks, theatres, restaurants, stores, hotels and much more. They had signs that read for Whites and Colored only.

Restaurant with separate entrances for Whites and Blacks, 1940
(Fig. 3, Source: Jack Delano/Library of Congress)

This period was called Jim Crow. Racism was visible, bold and violent.

The Civil Rights Act was signed in 1965. It abolished segregation but to this day racism continues.

There were over 4,000 Blacks lynched between 1619 and the present.[17] Many were lynched on church grounds right after church service. Whites took pictures of themselves next to the Black lynched victim. They viewed lynchings as going to a picnic or a circus.

Crowd smiles, lynching of Lige Daniels, 1920
(Fig. 4, Source: *Without Sanctuary*)

There were hundreds of White females who lied and accused Black males of rape. One of the worst happened on May 31, 1921 in Tulsa, Oklahoma. Dick Rowland was 19. Sarah Page was 17. Sarah was in the elevator and Dick tripped entering the elevator. He accidentally bumped into Sarah. She accused him of rape.

Blacks had done very well in spite of racism in Tulsa. People called the Black neighborhood Black Wall Street. Blacks owned thousands of houses, over 150 businesses, which included thirty grocery stores and numerous other stores, including clothing and jewelry, twenty-one restaurants, three hotels, two movie theatres, a bank, hospital and much more.[18]

This was the first time in American history where a U.S. city was bombed by its own government. The police worked with the White mob. The fire department did nothing. The insurance companies denied all claims. Thousands of Blacks were left homeless. Reparations were never given.

Whites were jealous of Black success. They used Sarah's lie to destroy Black Wall Street and kill 26 Blacks.

Another was the tragedy to Emmett Till in August 1955.[19] He was 14 years of age visiting Mississippi. He went into a grocery store and was accused by Carolyn Bryant of whistling at her. Two White men beat him then shot him. They then threw him in a river. Carolyn later denied her story. The two men were indicted, but never convicted. After the trial, they admitted their guilt.

Emmett's mother wanted the world to see hatred, racism and injustice. She had Emmett put in an open casket. She asked as many newspapers, magazines, radio and television stations to show the world how they mutilated her son.

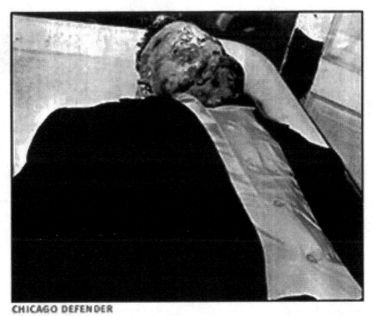

CHICAGO DEFENDER

Body of Emmett Till, 1955 (Fig. 5, Source: *Chicago Defender* archives)

This inspired Rosa Parks in December 1955 to sit in the front of the bus. This motivated Dr. Martin Luther King and sparked the Civil Rights Movement.

Some would say slavery ended in 1865. Some would say lynchings ended in 1968. Others would say Blacks became empowered in 1965 with the Civil Rights legislation.

Let me show the connection between Dick Rowland in Tulsa, 1921; Emmett Till in Mississippi, 1955; and George Floyd in Minneapolis, 2020.

On May 25, 2020, the Minneapolis police accused Floyd of using a counterfeit bill. The police officer, Derek Chauvin handcuffed Floyd and forced him to the ground. He then placed his foot on his neck for 8 minutes and 46 seconds. I want you to find a way of honoring George Floyd for 8 minutes and 46 seconds.

Floyd kept pleading to the officer, "I can't breathe." He died while three other officers did nothing.

Police kneels on neck of George Floyd (Fig. 6, Source: Witness camera)

Hundreds of Black people have been murdered by police. What made this murder different? It was caught on camera and shown worldwide. Your mobile device is your weapon and form of self-defense.

This is an example of White privilege. To be aware of a wrong, but do nothing about it. They rationalize because they did not have their knee on Floyd they are exempt of any crime.

During slavery, only 27 percent of Whites in the South were slave owners.[20] The majority of Whites, 73 percent, allowed slavery to continue. Does their silence exempt them from allowing slavery to continue?

I want you to read about the White Quakers who fought against slavery.

Do you really think Hitler killed six million Jews? The larger German population allowed it to happen. Racism cannot persist without White privilege, silence and complicity.

Lynching was not reserved for Black males. Hundreds of Black women were also lynched. In Georgia in 1918, Mary Turner was eight months pregnant. She was brutally lynched and her baby was ripped out of her with a knife. The Mary Turner Project[21] was created so we would never forget the ugliness of racism.

On September 15, 1963, members of the 16th Street Baptist Church in Birmingham were worshiping God. Four members of the Ku Klux Klan used 15 sticks of dynamite and blew up the church. Four girls died. They include Addie Collins (age 14), Cynthia Wesley (age 14), Carole Robertson (age 14) and Carol McNair (age 11).[22]

Clockwise from top left,
Addie Mae Collins, Cynthia Wesley,
Carole Robertson and Denise McNair
(Fig. 7, Source: National Park Service)

Racism is a mental health disorder. It is perpetuated by psychopaths who have no remorse. How do you lynch anyone? How do you celebrate lynching after church? How do you bomb a church and kill four little girls?

I want you to read about Frederick Douglass. He was born in 1818. He was born into slavery. It was illegal for Blacks to read. Douglass realized reading must be a powerful weapon. He would sneak out at night with a candle and a book. He was determined to learn how to read. Many times, his owner would catch and beat him. This inspired Douglass even more.[23]

Do you like to read? Do you value education? What is your GPA? Why do you think Whites did not want Blacks to be educated? Why do you think they wanted separate schools? Why do you think they required a literacy test before you could vote?

I want you to read Douglass' speech about July 4th.[24] How can racist advocate for freedom for everyone except Blacks? The Declaration of Independence read, "all men are created equal." What was the status of Blacks on July 4, 1776? What was our status in 1787? Racists decided we were 3/5 of a person.

Racism is very consistent. We were viewed as 3/5 of a person in 1787 and to this day, Blacks only earn 3/5 (60 percent) of White male income. All the marches, protests, legislation, court decisions and apologies have not changed this racist phenomenon.

Douglass had major concerns with President Abraham Lincoln. Did Lincoln really free the slaves or did he save the Union? What is the difference between the Emancipation Proclamation and the Thirteenth Amendment?

Why are so many White Southerners in love with the Confederate flag? Why is it a symbol of pride for so many Whites and a symbol of a terrible past for so many Blacks? Is the South still angry that they lost the Civil War? How can you have one country and two flags? The Confederate flag is displayed at meetings of White hate groups. There are over 200 of these groups.[25] The two largest are the Ku Klux Klan and the skinheads. They all love the Confederate flag. It is proudly displayed on the grounds in front of the capitol in southern states. Some Whites believe America was great before the South lost the war.

Speaking of the South, have you ever heard of the Tuskegee Experiment?[26] I want you to research it, write a paper and have a debate.

The United States Public Health Service and Tuskegee Institute started the experiment in 1932. Six hundred Black men were promised free medical care. They were not told that 399 had syphilis. They went untreated for 40 years. Penicillin was available in 1947 which cures syphilis, but was never given to the men. They infected their wives and their children. In 1997, President Clinton apologized, but reparations were never given.

How many Blacks were killed in Africa by Whites? How many were killed in the slave dungeons? How many died on the slave ships? How many died on the plantations? The estimated percentage is 20. The estimated number is ten million.[27] The African word for "holocaust" is Maafa. We must never forget those who died. I respect all those who refused to be enslaved. I also understand and appreciate all those who survived the dungeons, ships and the plantations because they wanted a better life for you and me.

WE ARE THE OFFSPRING OF THE ANCESTORS WHO WOULD NOT DIE!

Do your textbooks mention that Blacks fought against slavery? They refused to work, broke tools, ran away and started over 265 revolts. I want you to read about Nat Turner, Denmark Vesey, Harriet Tubman and many others. These revolts killed White owners and Africans ran to freedom. We do not need any more teachers having a class play on docile Blacks accepting slavery. We need plays showing strong assertive Blacks resisting slavery.

We also need teachers starting Black history on pyramids in Egypt in 2780 B.C.[28] and not plantations in the South in 1619.

Black children are tired of talking about slavery and how we accepted it. We need more information about the pyramids and slave revolts and less about accepting slavery.

Racism has tried to make Blacks feel inferior. During slavery on the plantations there could be 100 Blacks, two White owners and a few White overseers with guns. Whites were always worried Blacks would revolt, break tools or work slower.

They felt a need to make Blacks hate themselves, despise their dark skin, broad nose and thick lips. They felt if they could reduce their unity, divide and conquer and make them look for differences, they could control them.

I want you to read the following letter supposedly written by Willie Lynch in 1712.[29] Regardless of the authenticity, I believe we can learn lessons from the letter.

Gentlemen, I greet you here on the banks of the James River in the year of our Lord one thousand seven hundred and twelve. First, I shall thank you, the gentlemen of the Colony of Virginia for bringing me here. I am here to help you solve some of your problems with slaves. Your invitation reached me on my modest plantation in the West Indies were I have experimented with some of the newest and still the oldest methods for control of slaves. Ancient Rome would envy us if my program is implemented.

As our boat sailed south on the James River, named for our Illustrious King, whose version of the Bible we cherish, I saw enough to know your problem is not unique. While Rome used cords of wood as crosses for standing human bodies along its old highways in great numbers, you are here using the tree and rope on occasion. I caught the whiff of a dead slave hanging from a tree a couple of miles back. You are not only losing valuable stocks by hangings, you are having uprisings, slaves are running away, your crops are sometimes left in the fields too long for maximum profit, you suffer occasional fires, your animals are killed. Gentlemen, you know what problems are; I do not need to elaborate. I am not here to enumerate your problems; however, I am here to introduce you to a method of solving them.

In my bag here, I have a foolproof method for controlling your Black slaves. I guarantee every one of you that if it is installed correctly, it will control the slaves for at least 300 years. My method is simple. Any member of your family or your overseer can use it. I have outlined a number of DIFFERENCES among the slaves, and I take these differences and make them bigger. I use FEAR, DISTRUST, and ENVY for control purposes. These methods have worked on my modest plantation in the West Indies and it will work throughout the South. Take this simple little list of differences, and think about them.

On the top of my list is "AGE" but it is there only because it starts with an "A": the second is "COLOR' or SHADE, there is INTELLEGENCE, SIZE, SEX, SIZE PLANTATIONS, STATUS ON PLATATION, ATTITUDE OF OWNERS, WHETHER THE SLAVES LIVE IN THE VALLEY, ON THE HILL, EAST, WEST, NORTH, SOUTH, HAVE FINE HAIR, COURSE HAIR, OR IS TALL OR SHORT. Now that you have a list of differences, I shall give you an outline of action – but before that I shall assure you that DISTRUST is stronger than TRUST, and ENVY is stronger than ADULATION, RESPECT, OR ADMIRATION. The Black salve [sic] after receiving this indoctrination shall carry on and will become self refueling and self generation for hundreds of years, maybe thousands.

Don't forget, you must pitch the OLD BLACK MALE vs. the YOUNG BLACK MALE and the YOUNG BLACK MALE against the OLD BLACK MALE. You must use the Dark Skin Slaves vs. the Light Skin Slaves and the Light Skin Slaves vs. the Dark Skin Slaves. You must use the Female vs. the Male, and the Male vs. the Female. You must also have your white servants and overseers Distrust all Blacks, but it is necessary your slaves trust and depend on us. The must love, respect, and trust only us. Gentlemen, these kits are the keys to control. Use them. Have your wives and children use them, never miss an opportunity. If used intensively for one year, the slaves themselves will remain perpetually distrustful. Thank you, gentlemen.

The letter said this self-hatred could last 300 years. It should have expired in 2012. Is it still going on today? I want you to write a paper, titled, "Are Blacks still suffering from the legacy of Willie Lynch?"

This has led many Blacks to suffer from Post-Traumatic Slavery Disorder (PTSD). When slavery ended, every Black person should have received racial counseling and therapy. As a result of not receiving counseling and therapy, many Blacks are suffering from PTSD.

Have you ever heard someone say, "being smart is acting White?" Have you ever heard a White student accuse another White student that being smart is acting Black? Why not? Why is speaking standard English speaking White?

Why is being in gifted and talented, honors or advanced placement classes acting White? Have you ever been recommended for those classes, but declined because you wanted to stay Black with your homies? Were you ever in one of those classes and a racist teacher was finally discussing a Black issue and wanted you to be the expert? Do you avoid answering or asking questions in class because you do not want to act White? Do you miss homework assignments for the same reason? Do you avoid extra credit projects?

This is called dumbing down. This will have long-term consequences on your career goals. Students who suffer from PTSD are dumbing down.

Beyoncé and 50 Cent sang a song titled, "Can't Leave Him Alone." I want you to listen to the lyrics and write a paper connecting the lyrics to PTSD. I also want you to identify five other songs released this year that promote PTSD.

I want you to watch the movie *Juice* starring Tupac and Omar Epps. There is a powerful scene where Tupac describes how much he hates himself and as a result he has no problem killing Omar.

I am very concerned about police brutality. The police kill over 1,000 citizens annually. Blacks are only 13 percent of the population, but are 33 percent of police fatalities. The police kill over 300 Blacks annually.[30] There are major protests when this happens. Do you have any idea how many Blacks kill each other annually? Almost 3,000. Where are the protests for the 3000 that we kill? Do Black Lives Matter when we kill each other? Blacks have killed more Blacks in one year than in the history of the Ku Klux Klan.

Do you know the number one killer in Black America? Is it heart disease, cancer, diabetes, homicide, drugs, AIDS or something else? What is it? Abortion.[31] Over 900 Black babies are killed daily. What does Black leadership say about that? Do Black Lives Matter if they are aborted?

Is this a form of PTSD? Why do we put more pressure on the police than ourselves? This reminds me of some students playing the race card with liberal White teachers. They try to convince the teacher to give them a higher grade because they are Black, poor and fatherless.

Jackie Robinson, Paul Robeson, Katherine Johnson, Mary Jackson, Dorothy Vaughan (females in the movie *Hidden Figures*) and numerous others did not play the race card.

They understood racism. They realized if they were inferior there was no need to discriminate. They realized hard work, a positive attitude, preparation and opportunity would produce success.

What is wrong with a Black student desiring to go to the museum? What is the problem with wanting to win the science fair, spelling bee or debate tournament?

When you suffer from PTSD you convince yourself that you are better in sports than science, music than math and rap than reading. What percent of the NBA and WNBA are Black? What percent of the doctors are Black?

Earlier in the book, I mentioned terms like good hair, pretty eyes and the brown bag test. Do you believe you are either beautiful or handsome? What is your definition of beauty? People who suffer from PTSD possess a White definition of beauty. They will say, "She is really pretty to be so dark."

What is blackface?

Minstrel show poster, 1900 (Fig. 8, Source: Strobridge Litho Co.)

It is an exaggerated form of makeup used in minstrel, theatre and comedy. You can still see blackface at Halloween and on college campuses. It makes Africans look as black as possible. Do you remember the four benefits of dark skin? Never forget them because racism and the media will do everything possible to convince you that you are ugly and inferior.

They will use terms like blackball, blacklisted, dark continent, dark horse, behind the eight ball (which is black), a little white lie, black sheep, and blackmail. Please provide five more.

Why was Malcolm Little so affected by the expectations of his teacher? Research shows White youth value more the expectations of their parents, media and society than their teacher. Black youth value more the expectations of their teachers. Why?

Does your teacher have high expectations for you? Are they recommending you for gifted, honors or advanced classes?

Has your teacher ever used the term "third world"? What comes to your mind when you hear this term? If there is a third world, there must be a first and second. What makes America first? Who leads the world in incarceration, drug usage, homicide, gun ownership, suicide, divorce, cancer, heart disease, pornography and much more? Who is second?

What comes to your mind when you hear Africa? Positive or negative thoughts? During slavery, we were taught to hate Africa. The people live in huts, walk through jungles and eat porridge. The media loves showing starving Black children. They have not contributed anything intellectually to improve society.

Whites in America love to return home by traveling to Europe. Do Blacks feel the same way about Africa? How many Blacks do you know who have visited Africa? From what country in Africa were your ancestors taken? Are there luxury hotels in Africa? How can I avoid being sick or dying in Africa?

I want you to save your money and visit Egypt and Ghana. I want you to see before the ancient Greek civilization, there was Egypt. The first university was in Egypt. Imhotep was the first doctor and Ahmose was the first mathematician.

I want you to see the pyramids built in 2780 B.C. This was 2,000 years before ancient Greek civilization. They are one of the seven wonders of the world and the only one still standing. They are 48 stories high and 755 feet wide. Africans were brilliant in math and science. What are your grades in math and science?

I also want you to visit Ghana. I want you to tour the slave dungeons. We entered the dungeons as Africans and after being taught to hate Africa, we exited the dungeons hating the color of our skin and the texture of our hair. We were taught we were inferior to Whites. We were taught not to like or trust one another.

How were Europeans able to invade Africa? How was a minority able to conquer a majority? How were Whites able to make them slaves? How were they able to take Africa's gold, diamonds, oil and much more? I would like you to research these questions and write a paper. I will give you some clues. Africans treated Whites with kindness. They did not realize the Whites had negative motives. Whites took advantage of Blacks' lack of unity. There were hundreds of Black groups.

Blacks used their intellect to build pyramids, temples and universities, but had nothing to defeat Europeans' guns. Africans had servants and Europeans convinced them that slavery would be similar to servanthood. Africans had no idea they would never see their relatives again. They had no idea that slavery included torturing, rape and lynchings. Servanthood was temporary, while slavery was permanent.

During slavery in America, there were four million enslaved Africans in 1860. There were 500,000 Blacks who were free. There were 4,000 Blacks who owned slaves.[32] Most of the ownership were relatives they were trying to protect.

In some schools, the self-hatred is so pronounced, Blacks fight over you stepped on my shoe, brushed up against me in a crowded hallway, made a negative comment on social media and much more. This began in 1619 in the dungeon, on the slave ship and on the plantation.

Many psychologists believe the best way to heal is to return to the original scene of the crime. PTSD began in the dungeons and it continues to this day.

Let us now talk about the controversial N word. There are books written about this one word. I encourage you to read them. There are college classes taught on this one word. Some rappers have made a distinction between "nigger" and "nigga." The latter is viewed as a term of endearment. I appreciate trying to turn a lemon into lemonade. Some rappers cannot make a song without using the N word.

My first question is why are Blacks upset when Whites use either word? Do Blacks know enough about their history to deny Whites from using either word? What does Black history teach us about this word?

I would like you to read slave narratives. I would like you to read how Whites used this word to destroy Black self-esteem. The word was ugly, violent and brutal. It was the worst word you could ever use against a person.

I want you to ask Harriet Tubman, Nat Turner and all your ancestors how they felt about the N word. It has been written, "If you truly knew what the word nigger meant to your ancestors, you would never use it."[33] They had the same feelings about the Confederate flag. They saw the N word and the flag as racist symbols that should be abolished.

Can you stop using the N word? Can you write letters to rappers asking them to stop? Can you write letters to radio stations asking them not to play any song using the N word? The slogan is Black Lives Matter. Not Niggas Matter.

Racists love using the term "culturally deprived." People who believe they are superior believe there is only one culture and anything different from White culture is inferior and therefore deprived.

The definition of culture is *lifestyle*. Everyone has a lifestyle and a culture. One culture is not better than another. Some schools think they are doing Blacks a favor allocating one day in February to eat fried chicken, macaroni and cheese and watermelon with gangster rap music playing.

Culture is much more than diet and music. It includes your spirituality, values, history, family, economics, politics, traditions, holidays and much more.

Frederick Douglass once said, "Power concedes nothing without a struggle." What does that quote mean to you? I want you to write a paper and provide concrete examples.

Douglass also wrote a speech about how Blacks felt about July 4, 1776. I want you to read the speech. Blacks were not free in 1776. There was no independence for them.

I also want you to read the British law case of the slave James Somerset.[34] There were British who owned plantations or had jobs in America and were also slave owners. When they took trips to England they brought their household slaves with them and used them to do unpaid household work. James Somerset tried to escape from slavery on one such trip but was recaptured. The judge ruled in 1772 that England would not send James back into slavery. This worried America which was a British colony. This was another reason why America went to war against England.

I want you to read the Emancipation Proclamation. Did it free any Blacks in the North? Did President Lincoln have any authority over southern states that had seceded from the Union? There were 620,000 deaths in the Civil War. A war over slavery and racism

I also want you to read the Thirteenth Amendment. It freed the slaves unless they committed a crime. SLAVERY NEVER ENDED. IT WAS REPLACED WITH SHARECROPPING AND INCARCERATION. In 1865, there were four million slaves who were paid nothing. Today, there are over two million inmates who are paid less than a dollar per hour.

I want you to watch the movies or TV programs *13, 12 Years a Slave, Roots, Amistad, Eyes on the Prize, Orange is the New Black, Hidden Figures, Glory, I am not your Negro, Just Mercy, Selma, 42, The Great Debaters, Malcolm X* and many more.

I want you read and write about Nat Turner, Martin Delaney, Paul Cuffe, Frederick Douglass, Marcus Garvey, Booker T. Washington, W.E.B. Du Bois, Martin Luther King Jr., Malcolm X, Stokely Carmichael, Medgar Evers, Thurgood Marshall, Al Sharpton, Jesse Jackson Sr., Louis Farrakhan, John Lewis, Harriet Tubman, Sojourner Truth, Fannie Lou Hamer, Ida B.Wells, Rosa Parks, Mary McLeod Bethune, Ella Baker, Dorothy Height, Daisy Bates, Shirley Chisholm, Ruby Bridges, Madam C. J. Walker and many more.

I also want you to read and write about Black billionaires and those very close to being billionaires. Who are they? How did they overcome racism? What are they doing to empower the Black community?

How did President Obama become the first Black president? What racist obstacles did he encounter? Please read and write a paper.

I want you to read the following legal cases: Fugitive Slave Act of 1850, Dred Scott 1857, the Compromise of 1877, *Plessy v. Ferguson 1896, Brown v. the Board of Education of Topeka 1954* and the Civil Rights Act of 1965.

I also want you to read about the Little Rock Nine, Freedom Riders, NAACP, Urban League, SCLC, SNCC, Nation of Islam, Black Panther Party, National Action Network, Rainbow PUSH, Color of Change, Black Lives Matter and other Black organizations.

I also want you to read and write about J. Edgar Hoover, COINTELPRO, the Trilateral Commission, Kalief Browder and the Central Park Five.

I want you to read and write a paper about Historically Black Colleges and Universities (HBCU). The first was Cheyney University, founded in 1837.[35] White universities did not admit Black students and some resisted until 1965.

HBCUs only have 10 percent of Black college students but produce over 20 percent of Black college graduates.[36] They also produce a greater percentage of graduate degree earners, lawyers and doctors. I encourage you to enroll in an HBCU. You will experience a larger number of Black professors and less racism.

There have been thousands of conversations, meetings, workshops and conferences on racism, race relations, diversity, equity and multiculturalism, but very little changes. Why? Because Whites do not want to share power and money.

Ask your teacher, principal and superintendent what percent of the students are Black? Then ask what percent of the school budget goes to Black businesses? If the budget percentage is lower than the population, then ask the superintendent when will they increase the budget to Black businesses? If you want to get to the root of an issue, follow the money.

A mayoral candidate promised if she won, each ward would receive 1/50 (there were fifty wards in the city) of the $3 billion budget. Does that sound fair? The problem was Whites only had 16 wards, but had $2 billion of the budget. How much were Whites going to lose?

Whites do not have a problem with meetings and singing songs as long as they control the money.

Dr. Frances Welsing, a brilliant psychiatrist, would often say, "Until you understand white supremacy, everything else will confuse you."[37] I would like you to write a paper about that quote. In order to defeat an enemy, you must understand how they think and what they value.

In order to overcome racism, we must view it like a chess game. We must be able to predict our opponents' moves.

Whites control 90 percent of the wealth in America. They achieved this wealth by raping Africa of its natural resources. They own this wealth by forcing millions of Africans to work for free from 1619 to 1865. There were over five million Blacks working as slaves in 1865.[38] They moved from slavery to sharecropping. Whites overcharged Blacks for land, seed and tools and underpaid them for the harvest. Blacks were always in debt.

They own this wealth because Blacks are only paid 60 percent of White male income.[39] They own this wealth because banks denied Blacks mortgage and business loans.

They own this wealth because there is inadequate transportation from the inner city to affluent suburbs that have more employment opportunities.

Your race or ethnicity should not determine the quality of air you breathe or the quality of water you drink. I want you to read and write about environmental racism, toxic waste, pollution and lead poisoning in the water.

They own this wealth because Black students have received an inferior education.

People who benefit from White privilege say, "I did not rape Africa, own slaves, or redline mortgages and business loans." They simply inherited their wealth.

Let me be clear. Not all Whites are wealthy. One percent of Whites own 50 percent of the wealth and 10 percent own 86 percent.[40] Forty percent each constitute the middle and working class. The remaining 10 percent live below the poverty line. There are actually more Whites below the poverty line (thirty million) than Blacks with ten million.[41]

For some strange reason, when the media does a poverty special, they can always find the ten million poor Blacks, but cannot find the thirty million poor Whites.

What is unfortunate, is the poor Whites believe they have more in common with the highest White 10 percent than with poor Blacks. Why?

When slavery ended in 1865, what were we given for 246 years of free labor? We were promised 40 acres and a mule,[42] but that never happened. The North knew the South was not going to agree to give land to Blacks.

How does White America feel about reparations? Have you ever heard of this term? I want you to write a paper on reparations and House of Representatives bill HR 40. It has died in the House since 1989. Only 15 percent of Whites are in favor of awarding reparations to Blacks. Seventy-four percent of Blacks are in favor of reparations.[43] This is clearly a divisive issue. The media loves displaying the 26 percent of Blacks against reparations, but they seldom interview the 74 percent majority in favor of reparations.

They also seldom interview the White 15 percent in favor of reparations. They love talking to the 85 percent against reparations.

Has America ever given reparations to anyone? Yes. In 1946, the federal government gave $1.3 billion plus land to 176 Native American groups.[44] In 1988, the federal government gave $40,000 each to 82,219 Asians for placing them in concentration camps between 1942 and 1945.[45]

Has America ever given reparations to Blacks? Yes. In 1923, a White woman in Rosewood, Florida, accused a Black man of rape. The Black town was destroyed and many Blacks were killed. In 1994, the lone nine survivors were given $150,000 and $500,000 was given to Black institutions.[46]

The city of Ashville North Carolina on July 13, 2020 apologized to the Black community. They promised they would try to close the wealth gap by providing more and better mortgage and business loans. I expect other cities to do similar. This is a start, but much more is needed.

When will America pay reparations to five million Blacks who worked for free from 1619 to 1865? When will America pay for Jim Crow discrimination from 1865 to the present?

Let me give you a math problem. What would be the cost if we used 1845 to 1865 for five million Blacks working six days a week for twelve hours at $10 per hour?

Some argue it was easier to pay nine Blacks, 176 Native American groups and 82,219 Asians than trying to figure out how to pay forty million Blacks who currently live in America.

I have a suggestion. Do not give any money to individuals. Give all the money to Black colleges, banks, radio and television stations and civil rights organizations. I would like for you to write a paper on this suggestion.

Remember power concedes nothing without a struggle. Power is synonymous with money. Only 15 percent of Whites are even willing to have a conversation on reparations much less pay trillions of dollars.

America does not have a problem with marches and discussions on racism as long as money does not need to be paid. How did Germany, South Africa and Canada address their racial problems?

Germany killed over six million Jews between 1941 and 1945. There was a war crimes trial and later, after East and West Germany reunified, the German government created a Truth and Reconciliation Commission in 1992. They publicly apologized to Jews and other wartime victims of Germany and removed all Nazi symbols. They paid $4 billion in reparations. They financially support the maintenance and growth of Israel.[47]

South Africa operated a racist regime of apartheid from 1948 to 1995. They also created a Truth and Reconciliation Commission.[48] Thousands of Whites apologized for robbing, raping and murdering Blacks during hearings that took place between 1996 and 2003. The government awarded Blacks eighty-five million dollars.

In Canada, Whites felt the Aborigine population were culturally deprived. In the late nineteenth century through 1980, they took the children from their parents and placed them in White homes. Almost 100,000 children were affected.[49]

In 2008, Canada also created a Truth and Reconciliation Commission and paid Aborigines $2 billion, and provided the children and their parents with social and psychological support.

What can America learn from Germany, South Africa and Canada? I want you to write a paper. I also want you to write a letter to your congressperson and US senator asking them to create a Truth and Reconciliation Commission.

In all three countries, the movement was led by youth. You often hear elders say, "our youth are our future." I disagree. Our youth are our present. They have no fear and nothing to lose. They have new ideas and are not burdened with tradition and old habits that are no longer effective.

Youth love technology because it is always changing. During the Civil Rights era, leaders needed days, weeks and months to organize a march in one city. Presently, with social media young people can post the date, time and location and within minutes in hundreds of cities, thousands of people are marching.

Elders could learn from youth and youth can learn from elders. To overcome racism, we need both respect and learning from each other. To overcome racism, we must implement four strategies:

Demonstrate

Boycott

Legislate

Enforcement

Let us review the above. Dr. Martin Luther King said, "Riots [Demonstrating, marching and protesting] are the language of the unheard."[50] What does this quote mean? Have you ever participated in a march? Would you like to participate in a march?

DEMONSTRATE

I want you to read and watch a video on the March from Selma to Montgomery, Alabama, in March 1965. I also want you to write a paper. The march started with 600 people who believed in nonviolence. The Constitution allowed for peaceful protest. They were confronted on March 7 at the Pettus Bridge by state troopers, the KKK and an angry mob displaying the Confederate flag, hollering the N word and barely holding back vicious dogs.

The march was called Bloody Sunday because the marchers were beaten terribly. The late Congressman, John Lewis was one of many beaten. I want you to write a paper about this brilliant activist.

Protesters taped the beating and mailed it to national television networks. America was embarrassed just like they were when George Floyd was murdered.

John Lewis (in raincoat, on the ground) and other protesters attacked by police, Bloody Sunday, 1965 (Fig. 9, Source: Politico)

The federal government on March 21, 1965 sent in the National Guard. The marchers had increased from 600 to 25,000 because of national media coverage. There were large numbers of Whites marching just like they did for George Floyd. They successfully made the 54-mile march. On August 6, 1965, President Lyndon Johnson signed the Voting Rights Act.

Your ancestors paid a heavy price for you not to use the N word. They paid a huge price for you to vote.

BOYCOTT

I want you to research the Montgomery Bus Boycott and write a paper. How long was the boycott? Was it successful? Should we do it again? Did we have more unity in 1955 than today? Would Blacks especially our youth be willing to boycott Nike, Apple, Amazon and others? What are the ten most popular companies for Black youth? Would they boycott them?

African Americans earn $1.3 trillion. We purchase over 25 percent of potato chips, soda pop, lard, cigarettes, liquor, movie tickets, music downloads, luxury cars, clothing, hair and skin care products, wigs, weaves and much more.[51]

Can you imagine the influence and leverage Blacks could have over these companies? There was a time when racists in Miami Beach discriminated against Jews. What was the Jewish response? They bought most of the luxury hotels and restaurants.

The owner of the NFL Washington Redskins, said he would never remove the racist name, Redskins. When corporations reacted to the Black Lives Matter protests and said they would remove sponsorships, the name was removed.

Remember, Frederick Douglass said, "Power concedes nothing without a struggle." Blacks must use their $1.3 trillion to fight against racism. What percent of the 1.3 trillion do Blacks spend with Black businesses? Three percent.[52] How much do they spend with White businesses? Over 90 percent. Are Blacks boycotting their own businesses? What percent of White income is spent with Black businesses? Less than 1 percent. This is the major issue never discussed at diversity, equity, inclusion and multicultural workshops. Why?

Remember Black Wall Street in Tulsa? How do we replicate it today? I want you to write a paper on how to replicate Black Wall Street.

LEGISLATE

You can march and boycott forever, but if the laws do not change then nothing happens. The late President Lyndon Johnson told Martin Luther King, "If you want the Civil Rights Bill put pressure on me."[53]

You cannot secure legislation if you are not registered to vote. Over fifty million Americans are not registered. Of those who are registered only 60 percent vote.[54] Racists will do everything possible to prevent people from voting. They will make you wait in line for hours. They will provide inferior equipment and inadequate training. They will close voting booths and make you travel for miles. They will make it difficult to vote absentee or early. They will deny inmates who have done their time to vote and will deny over two million inmates the right to participate in a democracy.

I want you to research voter suppression. Why do racists want to suppress your vote? What are the benefits for youth to vote? It could reduce or eliminate student loans. It could provide more college grants. It could provide more employment and recreation for youth. It could reduce if not eliminate police racial profiling and police brutality. It would allow you a greater chance to receive a fair trial because jurors must be registered. Would you want to be tried by twelve racists or a jury of your peers?

I want you to provide five or more benefits of voting.

ENFORCEMENT

This has always been the major challenge. How do schools remove racist, ineffective teachers who have low expectations for Black students? How do schools remove racist teachers who would rather suspend Black students or place them in special education? How do you enforce their removal if they have tenure? How do you enforce the above if the school district is controlled by unions? How do you enforce the above if the principal, superintendent and school board members are racist?

How do you stop racial profiling and police brutality if their commanders are racist? How do you stop the above if whistle blowers are fired? How do you stop the above if racist police officers are protected by unions? How do you stop the above if the district attorney is more loyal to police officers than citizens? How do victims of police brutality secure justice if the jury and judge are racist?

How do Blacks secure equal housing, employment, mortgages and business loans if the above executives are racist?

We can demonstrate and legislate forever, but without enforcement we are still waiting hours to vote. We can demonstrate and legislate forever, but Blacks will have smaller numbers in gifted and talented classes and greater numbers in suspension, special education and remedial classes. We can demonstrate and legislate forever, but racist police officers will still be exonerated by racist jurors and judges. We can demonstrate and legislate forever, but racist executives will still deny housing, employment, mortgages and business loans.

I recommend every educator, police officer, judge, employer, loan officer and anyone with authority and influence take mandatory training on equity and diversity.

How do we secure enforcement? We must leverage our economic power. The only thing a racist understands is economic power. We must boycott White businesses. We must support more Black businesses. We must recreate Black Wall Street. We must demand our fair share of city, state and federal contracts.

How do we secure enforcement? We must understand racism is a spiritual demon. We must fight this demon spiritually. We must pray. Dr. King taught us not to hate and instead to walk in love.

How do Blacks overcome racism? I suggest the Nguzo Saba. These are seven principles that are part of Kwanzaa created by Dr. Maulana Karenga.[55]

The Nguzo Saba – Seven Principles

1. UMOJA (UNITY) To strive for and maintain unity in the family, community, nation and race.

2. KUJICHAGULIA (SELF-DETERMINATION) To define ourselves, name ourselves and speak for ourselves, instead of being defined and spoken for by others.

3. UJIMA (COLLECTIVE WORK AND RESPONSIBILITY) To build and maintain our community together and to make our brothers and sisters problems our problems and to solve them together.

4. UJAMAA (CO-OPERATIVE ECONOMICS) To build and maintain our own stores, shops and other businesses and to profit together from them.

5. <u>NIA</u> (PURPOSE) To make as our collective vocation the building and developing of our community in order to restore our people to their traditional greatness.

6. <u>KUUMBA</u> (CREATIVITY) To do always as much as we can, in the way we can in order to leave our community more beautiful and beneficial than when we inherited it.

7. <u>IMANI</u> (FAITH) To believe with all our heart in our parents, our teachers, our leaders, our people and the righteousness and victory of our struggle.

Blacks could overcome racism if we increased our unity. Stop gossiping, cursing, bullying, fighting and using the N word.

Blacks could overcome racism if we started our history on pyramids and not plantations. Do not use the word "can't." Try to be accepted in gifted and talented, honors and advanced placement classes. Believe that you excel in science, math and reading.

Blacks could overcome racism if we all volunteered a few hours a week. Do you study more than watch social media or surf the internet?

Blacks could overcome racism if we spent a minimum of 10 percent of our income with Black businesses. Consider starting a business. How much do you have in savings?

Blacks could overcome racism if we improved our grades and had higher career goals. Can you provide a different career for each letter of the alphabet? Please exclude sports and entertainment.

Blacks could overcome racism if we cleaned our houses and neighborhoods and made them beautiful.

Blacks could overcome racism if we improved our spirituality.

In closing, there has been a lot of concern about the phrase, "Black Lives Matter." Those Whites who do not see color and enjoy White privilege would rather say, "All Lives Matter." I agree All Lives Matter when Black Lives Matter. I agree to stop using Black Lives Matter when racism stops. Until then,

BLACK LIVES MATTER!

CELEBRATE BLACK HISTORY EVERY DAY

Third Monday in January   Birthday of Martin Luther King

February   Black History Month

February 4 Birthday of Rosa Parks

March ?   Birthday of Harriet Tubman

May 19 Birthday of Malcolm X

June 19 When all enslaved Africans knew they were free

August 17 Birthday of Marcus Garvey

December 26 – January 1 Kwanzaa

VOCABULARY

Write the definition for each word and create a sentence.

Melanin	Abolish
Complicity	Wealth
Perpetuated	Reparations
Phenomenon	Reconciliation
Maafa	Apartheid
Authenticity	Legislation
Holocaust	Democracy
Narrative	Tenure

QUESTIONS

What is the distinction between race and ethnicity?

What is the brown bag test?

What are four benefits of dark skin?

What is the difference between prejudice, discrimination and racism?

Why are Blacks more affected by teachers' expectations?

What is the conversation about the police?

What was Black Wall Street?

What do you know about the pyramids?

Why did Whites prevent Blacks from reading?

What was the number of slave revolts?

How many Africans died in the slave trade?

How did your ancestors feel about the N word?

What is PTSD?

What is dumbing down?

What is the leading killer in Black America?

Who was the first doctor?

How were Whites able to successfully invade Africa?

What is the difference between the Emancipation Proclamation and the Thirteenth Amendment?

COVID 1619 CURRICULUM

What do you know about reparations?

What is voter suppression?

What drives racism?

What are the four strategies to overcome racism?

What is the relationship between COVID 19 and COVID 1619?

NOTES

1. "On Views of Race and Inequality, Blacks and Whites Are Worlds Apart" (June 27, 2016), Pew Research Center, Social and Demographic Trends. https://www.pewsocialtrends. org/2016/06/27/on-views-of-race-and-inequality-blacks-and-whites-are-worlds-apart/

2. World Population Clock, 7.8 Billion People (2020), Worldometer. https://www.worldometers.info/world-population/

3. Frank W. Sweet, "One Drop Rule, AKA: Act 320 of 1911," *Encyclopedia of Arkansas*, last updated: February 1, 2019. https://encyclopediaofarkansas.net/entries/one-drop-rule-5365

4. Toshiko Taneda, Charlotte Greenbaum and Kelly Kline (July 10, 2020), "2020 World Population Data Sheet Shows Older Populations Growing, Fertility Rates Declining" Washington, DC: Population Reference Bureau. https://www.prb.org/2020-world-population-data-sheet/

5. Liz Droge-Young (June 24, 2016), "Darker Skin Is Stronger Skin, Says New View of Human Skin Color," Research News, University of California San Francisco. https://www.ucsf.edu/news/2016/06/403401/darker-skin-stronger-skin-says-new-view-human-skin-color

6. "The Significance of the 'Doll Test,'" NAACP Legal Defense Fund, accessed July 16, 2020. https://www.naacpldf.org/ldf-celebrates-60th-anniversary-brown-v-board-education/significance-doll-test/

7. Vernon C. Thompson (November 16, 1978), "Howard's Greek Clubs Offer Social Life to Commuter Students," *The Washington Post*. https://www.washingtonpost.com/archive/local/1978/11/16/howards-greek-clubs-offer-social-life-to-commuter-students/28ba959f-712f-4d9c-8f48-bebe885b03ca/

8. Travis Riddle and Stacy Sinclair (April 2, 2019), "Racial disparities in school-based disciplinary actions are associated with county-level rates of racial bias," *PNAS*. https://doi.org/10.1073/pnas.1808307116

9. Malcolm X (1965), *The Autobiography of Malcolm X: As Told to Alex Haley*, New York: Grove Press, 38.

10. Clare Lombardo, "Why White School Districts Have So Much More Money" (February 26, 2019), NPR. https://www.npr.org/2019/02/26/696794821/why-white-school-districts-have-so-much-more-money

11. Fair Housing Testing Program, U.S. Department of Justice, updated March 5, 2019. https://www.justice.gov/crt/fair-housing-testing-program-1

    "Fair Housing Testing in Chicago Finds Discrimination Based on Race and Source of Income" (January 28, 2019). National Low Income Housing Coalition. https://nlihc.org/resource/fair-housing-testing-chicago-finds-discrimination-based-race-and-source-income

12. Dionissi Aliprantis and Daniel R. Carroll (February 28, 2019), "What Is Behind the Persistence of the Racial Wealth Gap?" Federal Reserve Bank of Cleveland. DOI: 10.26509/frbc-ec-201903

13. Criminal Justice Fact Sheet (2020), NAACP. https://www.naacp.org/criminal-justice-fact-sheet/

14. "Implicit Bias: Recognizing the Unconscious Barriers to Quality Care and Diversity in Medicine" (January 24, 2020), *Cardiology Magazine*. https://www.acc.org/latest-in-cardiology/articles/2020/01/01/24/42/cover-story-implicit-bias-recognizing-the-unconscious-barriers-to-quality-care-and-diversity-in-medicine

    Khiara M. Bridges (Fall 2018), "Implicit Bias and Racial Disparities in Health Care" *Human Rights Magazine*, ABA.

https://www.americanbar.org/groups/crsj/publications/human_rights_magazine_home/the-state-of-healthcare-in-the-united-states/racial-disparities-in-health-care/

15. Drew Desilver, Michael Lipka and Dalia Fahmy (June 3, 2020), "Fact Tank: Ten things we know about race and policing in the U.S.," Pew Research Center. https://www.pewresearch.org/fact-tank/2020/06/03/10-things-we-know-about-race-and-policing-in-the-u-s/

16. Henry Louis Gates Jr. (2013), "How Many Slaves Landed in the U.S.?" *The African Americans: Many Rivers to Cross*, PBS.org, originally posted on The Root. https://www.pbs.org/wnet/african-americans-many-rivers-to-cross/history/how-many-slaves-landed-in-the-us/

17. Equal Justice Initiative (2007), *Lynching in America: Confronting the Legacy of Racial Terror*, Montgomery, AL. https://eji.org/reports/lynching-in-america/

    "There have been thousands of lynching victims in the U.S." (October 22, 2019), *The Washington Post.* www.washingtonpost.com/history/2019/10/22

18. Alexis Clark (September 4, 2019), "Tulsa's 'Black Wall Street' Flourished as a Self-Contained Hub in Early 1900s," History.com. https://www.history.com/news/black-wall-street-tulsa-race-massacre

19. "August 28, 1955, This Date in History: Emmett Till Is Murdered" (February 9, 2010), History.com. https://www.history.com/this-day-in-history/the-death-of-emmett-till#:~:text=August%2028-,Emmett%20Till%20is%20murdered,white%20woman%20four%20days%20earlier

20. Sarah Pruitt (May 3, 2016), "Five Myths about Slavery," History.com, updated June 23, 2020. https://www.history.com/news/5-myths-about-slavery

21. "Remembering Mary Turner" (2014), Valdosta, GA: The Mary

Turner Project. www.maryturner.org

22. Chelsey Parrot Sheffer, "16th Street Baptist Church Bombing," *Encyclopedia Brittanica*, last updated June 26, 2020. https://www.britannica.com/event/16th-Street-Baptist-Church-bombing

    "Four Little Girls," National Park Service, last updated March 23, 2016. https://www.nps.gov/articles/16thstreetbaptist.htm

23. Frederick Douglass (1845), *Narrative of the Life of Frederick Douglass, An American Slave*, Boston: Anti-Slavery Office.

24. Frederick Douglass (July 5, 1852), *What to the Slave Is the Fourth of July?* Speech to Rochester Ladies' Anti-Slavery Society.

25. David Klepper (June 5, 2020), "Facebook removes nearly 200 accounts tied to white supremacy groups looking to exploit protests," *USA Today*. https://www.usatoday.com/story/tech/2020/06/05/facebook-removes-nearly-200-accounts-tied-white-supremacy-groups/3160738001/

26. Elizabeth Nix, "Tuskegee Experiment: The Infamous Syphilis Study," History.com, originally published May 16, 2017, updated July 29, 2019. https://www.history.com/news/the-infamous-40-year-tuskegee-study

27. "Africans in America: The Middle Passage," Resource Bank: Teacher's Guide, PBS.org. https://www.pbs.org/wgbh/aia/part1/1p277.html

28. Anthropology Outreach Office, "The Egyptian Pyramid," National Museum of Natural History, Smithsonian Institution, revised February 2005. https://www.si.edu/spotlight/ancient-egypt/pyramid

29. "Is Willie Lynch's Letter Real?" (May 2004), Questions for the Museum. Big Rapids, MI: Jim Crow Museum of Racist

Memorabilia, Ferris State University. https://www.ferris.edu/ HTMLS/news/jimcrow/question/2004/may.htm

30. Amber Goodwin and Chico Tillmon (June 16, 2020), "Police kill 1,000 people a year with guns," THINK, NBC News. https://www.nbcnews.com/think/opinion/police-kill-1-000-people-year-guns-white-anti-gun-ncna1227536

Police Violence Map, Mapping Police Violence.org. https:// mappingpoliceviolence.org

31. Genocide: Black Abortions in America, Grand Rapids Right to Life. www.grrtl.org

National Center for Health Statistics (May 3, 2017), Health of Black or African American Non-Hispanic Population, Centers for Disease Control. https://www.cdc.gov/nchs/fastats/ black-health.htm

32. "Free-born," In *The Making of African American Identity, Volume I: 1500–1865* (June 2009), National Humanities Center. http://nationalhumanitiescenter.org/pds/maai/ identity/text3/text3read.htm

33. Brando Simeo Starko (May 18, 2017), "If you truly knew what the N-word meant to your ancestors, you'd NEVER use it," The Undefeated. https://theundefeated.com/features/if-you-truly-knew-what-the-n-word-meant-to-our-ancestors-youd-never-use-it/

34. Ruth D'Alessandro, et al., eds., "Slave or Free?" in Black Presence: Asian and Black History in Britain, an Exhibition in Partnership with the National Archives. https://www. nationalarchives.gov.uk/pathways/blackhistory/rights/ slave_free.htm#top

35. "Who We Are, The First HBCU," Cheyney University of Pennsylvania. https://cheyney.edu/who-we-are/the-first-hbcu/

36. Brian Bridges (2020), "African Americans and College Education by the Numbers," United Negro College Fund. https://uncf.org/the-latest/african-americans-and-college-education-by-the-numbers#:~:text=HBCUs%20make%20up%20only%20three,of%20all%20African%20American%20graduates.

37. Frances Cress Welsing (May 6, 2019), *Pushing Black*. Facebook Video. https://www.facebook.com/pushingblack/videos/until-you-understand-white-supremacy-everything-else-will-confuse-you-dr-frances/674915316272370/

38. History.com Editors, "Slavery in America" (November 12, 2009), A&E Television Network, last updated July 6, 2020. https://www.history.com/topics/black-history/slavery

39. Eileen Patten (July 1, 2016), "Fact Tank: Racial, Gender Wage Gaps Persist in the U.S., Despite Some Progress," Pew Research Center. https://www.pewresearch.org/fact-tank/2016/07/01/racial-gender-wage-gaps-persist-in-u-s-despite-some-progress/

40. Robert Frank (November 14, 2017), "Richest 1% now owns half the world's wealth," CNBC. https://www.cnbc.com/2017/11/14/richest-1-percent-now-own-half-the-worlds-wealth.html

41. Poverty Rate by Race/Ethnicity (2018), Kaiser Family Foundation. https://www.kff.org/other/state-indicator/poverty-rate-by-raceethnicity/?currentTimeframe=0&sortModel=%7B%22colId%22:%22Location%22,%22sort%22:%22asc%22%7D

42. Hannah Packman, "Juneteenth and the Broken Promise of 'Forty Acres and a Mule'" (June 19, 2020), National Farmers Union. https://nfu.org/2020/06/19/juneteenth-and-the-broken-promise-of-40-acres-and-a-mule/

43. Rachel Frazen (October 25, 2019), "Most Oppose Reparations for Slavery: Poll," The Hill. https://thehill.com/policy/

finance/467451-most-oppose-reparations-for-slavery-poll

44. Environment and Natural Resources Division, "Lead Up to the Indian Claims Commission Act of 1946," U.S. Department of Justice. Updated May 12, 2015. https://www.justice.gov/enrd/lead-indian-claims-commission-act-1946

45. Sharon Yamato (June 25, 2012), "Civil Liberties Act of 1988," *Densho Encyclopedia.* https://encyclopedia.densho.org/Civil_Liberties_Act_of_1988/

46. Jerry Fallstrom (April 9, 1994), "Senate OKs $2.1 Million for Rosewood Reparations," *South Florida Sun-Sentinel.* https://www.sun-sentinel.com/news/fl-xpm-1994-04-09-9404080701-story.html

47. Melissa Eddy (November 17, 2012), "For 60th Year, Germany Honors Duty to Pay Holocaust Victims," *The New York Times.* https://www.nytimes.com/2012/11/18/world/europe/for-60th-year-germany-honors-duty-to-pay-holocaust-victims.html#:~:text=Germany%27s%20postwar%20reparations%20program%20has,expand%20the%20guidelines%20for%20qualification.

Priscilla Hayner (2001), *Unspeakable Truths: Transitional Justice and the Challenge of Truth Commissions,* Psychology Press.

48. Truth and Reconciliation Commission (TRC) Report (2017), Truth and Reconciliation Commission of South Africa. https://www.justice.gov.za/trc

49. Truth and Reconciliation Commission of Canada: Calls to Action (2015), National Centre for Truth and Reconciliation. www.trc.ca

50. Lily Rothman (April 28, 2015), "What Martin Luther King Jr. Really Thought about Riots," *Time.* https://time.com/3838515/baltimore-riots-language-unheard-quote/

51. University of Georgia (March 21, 2019), "Minority Markets Have $3.9 Trillion Buying Power," Newswise. https://www.newswise.com/articles/minority-markets-have-3-9-trillion-buying-power

52. University of Georgia (March 21, 2019), "Minority Markets."

53. Ted Gittinger and Allen Fisher (Summer 2004), "LBJ Champions the Civil Rights Act of 1964," *Prologue Magazine*, National Archives. https://www.archives.gov/publications/prologue/2004/summer/civil-rights-act-1.html

54. Election Initiatives Project (June 21, 2017), "Why Are Millions of Citizens Not Registered to Vote?" Pew Trusts. https://www.pewtrusts.org/en/research-and-analysis/issue-briefs/2017/06/why-are-millions-of-citizens-not-registered-to-vote

55. Maulana Karenga (2008), "Kwanzaa: A Celebration of Family, Community and Culture," Los Angeles: University of Sankore Press. http://www.officialkwanzaawebsite.org

UPDATES